This Book Belongs to

_____

Thank you

To ensure that you have the best experience using this coloring book and to prevent bleeding, although the illustrations are on one-side, we recommend coloring using pencils.

If you are going to use any kind of ink that may cause bleeding through out the papers, we recommend tearing out the coloring pages or using a buffer page. (you can find blank buffer pages at the end of the book.)

COPYRIGHT
All rights reserved. This book or any portion of it may not be reproduced or used in any manner whatsoever without the express written permission of the author & the publisher except for the use of brief quotations in a book review. Licensed graphics used with all appropriate commercial licenses.
Although, the publisher and author have used their best efforts in writing and preparing this book, they make no representations or warranties with respect to the accuracy or completeness of the contents of this document. The information is to be used at your own risk. The author cannot guarantee any specific outcomes that may result from using the methods outlined in the following pages.

Color Testing Page

This page is intentionally left blank to avoid color bleeding.

Color Testing Page

This page is intentionally left blank to avoid color bleeding.

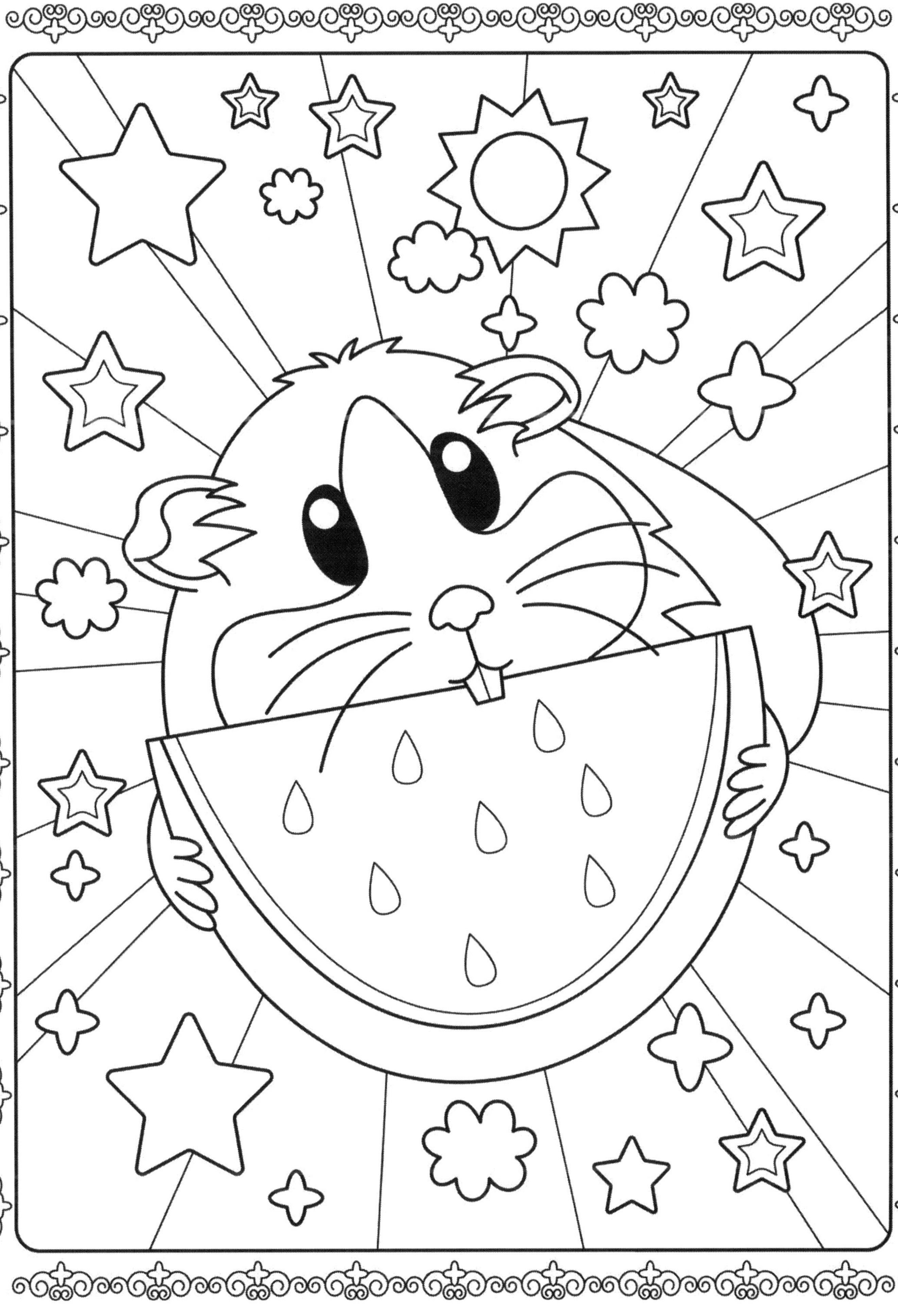

This page is intentionally left blank to avoid color bleeding.

This page is intentionally left blank to avoid color bleeding.

This page is intentionally left blank to avoid color bleeding.

This page is intentionally left blank to avoid color bleeding.

This page is intentionally left blank to avoid color bleeding.

This page is intentionally left blank to avoid color bleeding.

This page is intentionally left blank to avoid color bleeding.

This page is intentionally left blank to avoid color bleeding.

This page is intentionally left blank to avoid color bleeding.

This page is intentionally left blank to avoid color bleeding.

This page is intentionally left blank to avoid color bleeding.

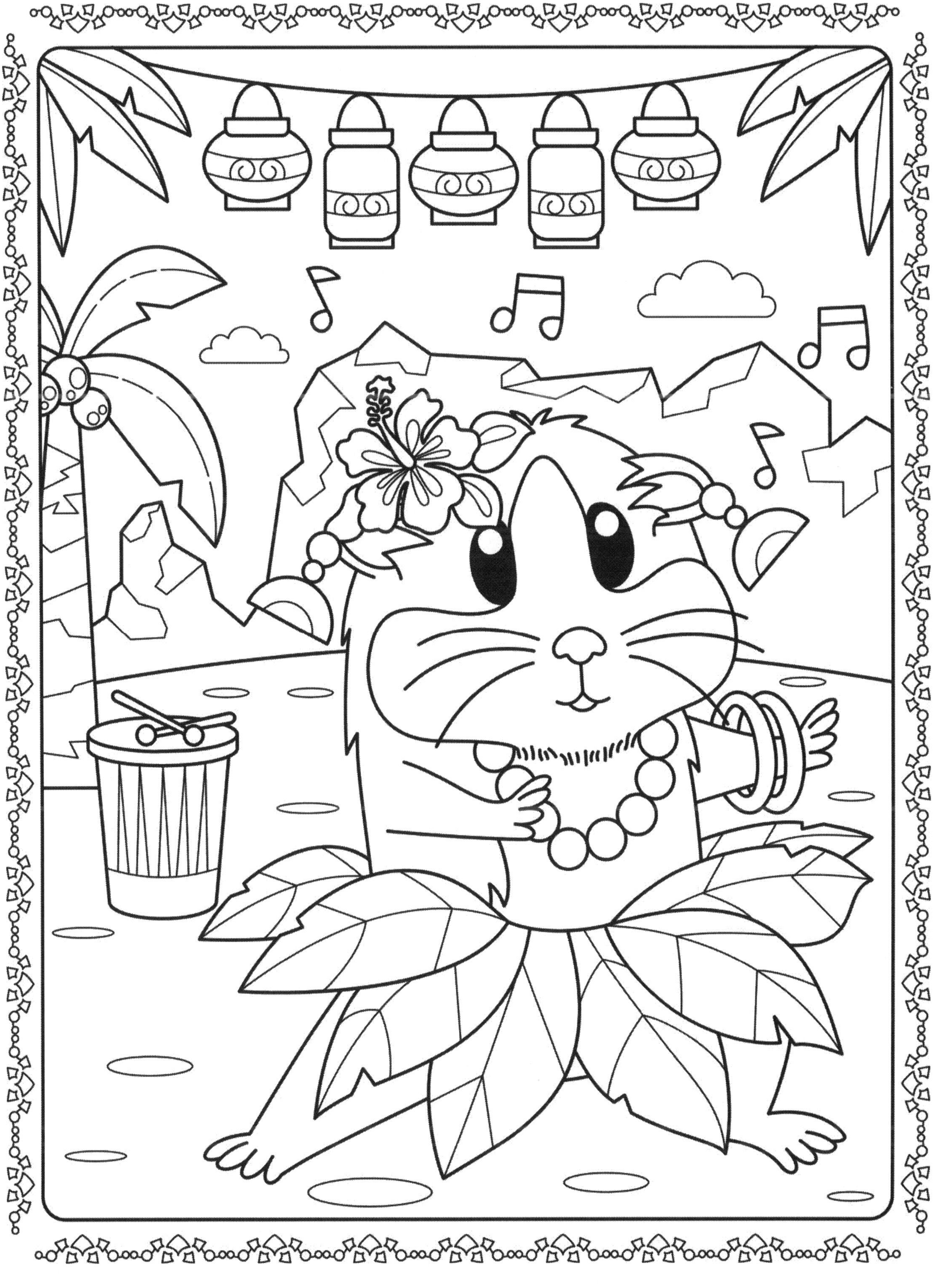

This page is intentionally left blank to avoid color bleeding.

This page is intentionally left blank to avoid color bleeding.

This page is intentionally left blank to avoid color bleeding.

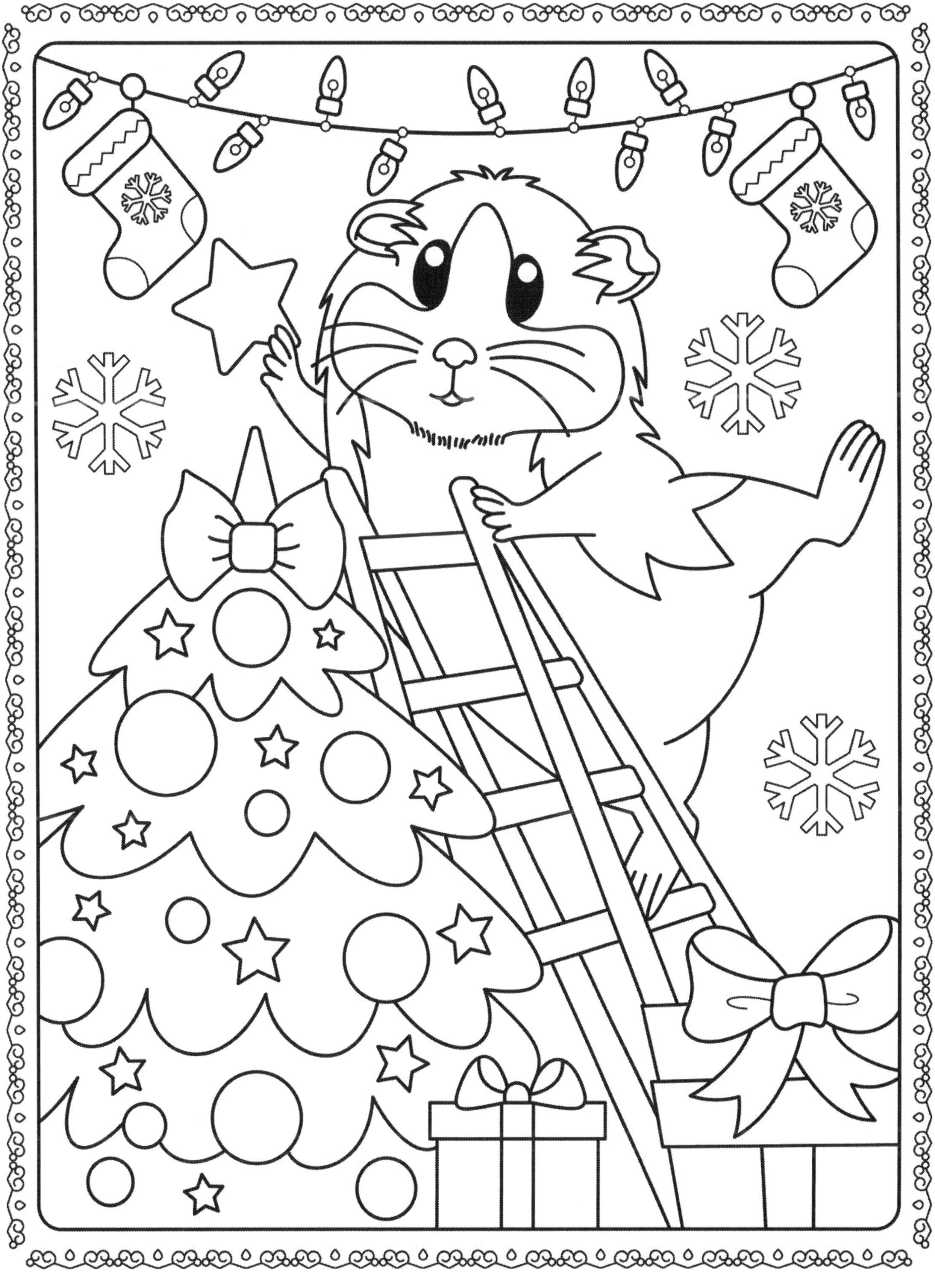

This page is intentionally left blank to avoid color bleeding.

This page is intentionally left blank to avoid color bleeding.

This page is intentionally left blank to avoid color bleeding.

This page is intentionally left blank to avoid color bleeding.

This page is intentionally left blank to avoid color bleeding.

This page is intentionally left blank to avoid color bleeding.

This page is intentionally left blank to avoid color bleeding.

This page is intentionally left blank to avoid color bleeding.

This page is intentionally left blank to avoid color bleeding.

This page is intentionally left blank to avoid color bleeding.

This page is intentionally left blank to avoid color bleeding.

TELEPHONE

This page is intentionally left blank to avoid color bleeding.

This page is intentionally left blank to avoid color bleeding.

This page is intentionally left blank to avoid color bleeding.

This page is intentionally left blank to avoid color bleeding.

This page is intentionally left blank to avoid color bleeding.

Buffer paper

Please cut and use between pages when you color
with any ink that may cause bleeding.

This Page is Intentionally Left Blank.

Buffer paper

Please cut and use between pages when you color
with any ink that may cause bleeding.

This Page is Intentionally Left Blank.

Printed in Great Britain
by Amazon